Native Americans

Researching American History

introduced and edited by

Pat Perrin and Arden Bowers

Assiniboin camp, 1833 drawing by Carl Bodmer (Smithsonian collection)

Discovery Enterprises, Ltd.
Carlisle, Massachusett

First Edition © Discovery Enterprises, Ltd., Carlisle, MA 2000

ISBN 1-57960-063-8

Library of Congress Catalog Card Number 00-103462

10   9   8   7   6   5   4   3   2   1

Printed in the United States of America

Subject Reference Guide:

Title: *Native Americans*
Series*: Researching American History*
introduced and edited by Pat Perrin and Arden Bowers

Nonfiction
Analyzing documents re: Native Americans

Credits:

Cover illustration: "Moving village," from Mediasource.

Other illustrations: Credited where they appear in the book.

Special Thanks to:

Karin Luisa Badt, editor of
Indians of the Southwest and *Indians of the Northeast*
Kevin P. Supples, editor of
Indians of the Great Plains
Rochelle Cashdan, editor of
Indians of the Northwest
and to Madeleine Meyers, editor of
The Cherokee Nation: Life Before the Tears

*All of which are published by Discovery Enterprises, Ltd.
Their research and editing all helped to make this book possible.*

Contents

About the Series

Researching American History is a series of books which introduces various topics and periods in our nation's history through the study of primary source documents.

Reading the Historical Documents

On the following pages you'll find words written by people during or soon after the time of the events. This is firsthand information about what life was like back then. Illustrations are also created to record history. These historical documents are called **primary source materials**.

At first, some things written in earlier times may seem difficult to understand. Language changes over the years, and the objects and activities described might be unfamiliar. Also, spellings were sometimes different. Below is a model which describes how we help with these challenges.

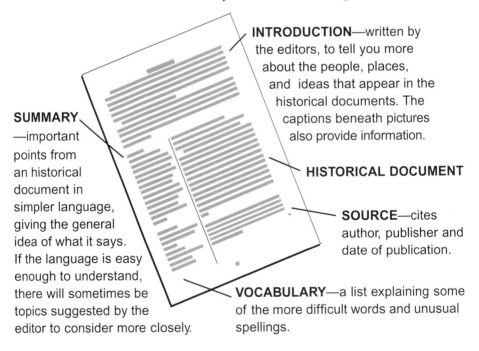

INTRODUCTION—written by the editors, to tell you more about the people, places, and ideas that appear in the historical documents. The captions beneath pictures also provide information.

SUMMARY—important points from an historical document in simpler language, giving the general idea of what it says. If the language is easy enough to understand, there will sometimes be topics suggested by the editor to consider more closely.

HISTORICAL DOCUMENT

SOURCE—cites author, publisher and date of publication.

VOCABULARY—a list explaining some of the more difficult words and unusual spellings.

In these historical documents, you may see three periods (...) called an ellipsis. It means that the editor has left out some words or sentences. You may see some words in brackets, such as [and]. These are words the editor has added to make the meaning clearer. When you use a document in a paper you're writing, you should include any ellipses and brackets it contains, just as you see them here. Be sure to give complete information about the author, title, and publisher of anything that was written by someone other than you.

Introduction:
Native Americans

by

Pat Perrin

When Europeans first came to the American continent, millions of people already lived here. Their ancestors had come here at least 20,000 years ago— and perhaps more than twice that long ago. They crossed over from Asia by a bridge of dry land that once connected Siberia and Alaska.

For people traveling on foot, this land was huge. The early people settled down in various areas, developing different customs and languages.

In 1492, Christopher Columbus made his way to a Caribbean island. By then, there were 2,000 or more different cultures in the New World. (Culture refers to a group—such as a nation—with similar beliefs and behaviors.) However, Columbus thought he had reached the East Indies (Asia), and so, he mistakenly called the people he met Indians.

Other Europeans repeated his error. Like their Asian ancestors, the native people all had dark eyes. Their dark hair could grow very long. Their skin tones varied. The Europeans called all the native people Indians, in spite of their cultural differences.

Today, we usually refer to the original inhabitants of the United States as Native Americans. The term Indian is still used too.

Some selections in this book were written down by those who lived the stories. Other tales were passed down through families and recorded later. A few of stories were written by European settlers about their own experiences encountering the Native Americans.

You'll notice that the Native Americans named themselves in different ways. In some groups, children were named after whatever a parent or religious leader happened to see at a special ceremony. Such names include Black Elk, Standing Bear, and Lame Deer. Sometimes, as a child grew to adulthood, he or she was renamed. Some Indian names, such as Geronimo and Cochise, may be familiar to you from history books.

This book can only touch on the rich history of this country's first people. Today, some Native Americans still follow their ancient traditions. Others live in the mainstream culture.

How the World Began

People from all around the world have told stories about how their world began. These tales were passed down from parents to their children and became part of each culture's traditions.

In some Native American creation stories, the first people came from within Earth. In others, they fell from the sky or they lived in water. Animals, plants and humans helped each other to find their proper places on Earth.

Summary:

A powerful chief lived in the sky. A beautiful tree grew in the center of his land.

One day, the tree fell over and left a big hole in the ground. The chief's young wife dropped through the hole. As she began to fall, she grabbed a handful of seeds from the tree.

Below, was a land covered with water. The creatures who lived in the water saw the woman falling. They wanted to make room for her.

Vocabulary:

ancient = very old
clutched = held; gripped
uprooted = torn out; pulled up
youthful = young

Iroquois Creation Story
told by Joseph Bruchac (Iroquois)

Before this world came to be,
there lived in the Sky-World
an ancient chief.
In the center of his land
grew a beautiful tree…
From that beautiful tree,
all good things grew.

Then it came to be
that the beautiful tree
was uprooted and through
the hole it made in the Sky-World
fell the youthful wife
of the ancient chief,
a handful of seeds,
which she grabbed from the tree
as she fell, clutched in her hand.

Far below there were only water
and water creatures
who looked up as they swam.
"Someone comes," said the duck
"We must make room for her."
The great turtle swam up
from his place in the depths.
"There is room on my back,"
the great turtle said.

"But there must be earth
where she can stand," said the duck
and so he dove beneath the waters,
but he could not reach the bottom....

Finally the muskrat tried.
He dove as deeply as he could,
swimming until his lungs almost burst.
With one paw he touched the bottom,
and came up with a tiny speck
of earth clutched in his paw.

"Place the earth on my back,"
the great turtle said,
and as they spread
the tiny speck of earth it grew
larger and larger and larger
until it became the whole world.

Then two swans flew up
and between their wings
they caught the woman
who fell from the sky.
They brought her gently
down to the earth
where she dropped her handful
of seeds from the Sky-World.

Then it was, that the first plants grew
and life on this new earth began.

Source: Joseph Bruchac, storyteller, *Iroquois Stories:
Heroes and Heroines, Monsters and Magic*. Trumans-
burg, New York: The Crossing Press, 1985, pp 15-7.

Summary:
   Turtle swam up to offer space on his back.
   The creatures decided to dive into the deep water and bring up some earth for her to stand on. The duck tried to reach the mud at the bottom of the water, but he failed. [The loon and the beaver beaver also tried and failed.]
   Then, the muskrat dove. He brought up a tiny piece of mud and placed it on the turtle's back. The mud grew to become Earth.
   Two swans saved the falling woman by spreading their wings, catching her, and bringing her safely to land. The woman dropped the handful of seeds, which grew into the first plants on Earth.

Vocabulary:
speck = small bit; spot

According to some creation myths, deities work together to make the world and everything on it. In a Hopi story, Spider Woman makes animals out of clay and uses powerful magic to bring them to life. When she creates human beings, she and the sky-god Tawa sing them to life. Spider Woman is drawn on this clay disk. She is also called Spider Grandmother. (Courtesy of Art Resource)

Summary:

In the beginning there was nothing but a hazy mist. Three gods created Earth, stars, waters, and clouds. Two superhumans were on Earth and they became the parents of the Zunis.

Vocabulary:

dieties = gods
fog = a hazy mist
saliva = spit

Zuni Creation Story

In the beginning, there was only fog. In the above world, there were three gods: Awonawilona, the Creator of All, the Sun and the Moon. Below there were two superhumans, Shiwanni and his wife Shiwanokia.

These three gods created the present world. Awonawilona made clouds and waters with his breath; Shiwanni made the stars from the bubbles of his saliva; and Shiwanokia made Mother Earth with her saliva. The Zunis (the Ahiwi) are Shiwanni and Shiwanokia's children.

Source: Karin Luisa Badt, ed., *Indians of the Southwest.* Carlisle, MA: Discovery Enterprises, Ltd., 1996, pp. 7-8.

Seminole Creation Story

When the Creator, the Grandfather of all things, created the earth,... [He made] animals on all fours, animals with hooves, animals with paws, birds with claws, insects, reptiles.... Creator put all the animals in a large shell...." "When the timing is right," He told the animals, "the shell will open and you will all crawl out. ...[and] take your respective places...."

Alongside the shell stood a great tree. As time passed, the tree grew...[and] eventually a root cracked the shell.... Wind helped the Panther out first, the Panther thanked Wind for the honor. Next to crawl out was the Bird.... After that, other animals emerged...Bear, Deer, Snake, Frog, Otter. ...no one besides the Creator could even begin to count them all. All went out to seek their proper places on earth.

When the Creator saw that all was done, He decided to name the animals and put them into Clans. For being such a good companion, the Creator rewarded the Panther... "Your Clan will have the knowledge for making laws and for making the medicine which heals,".... Creator told the Wind: "You will serve all living things so they may breathe. Without the wind—or air—all will die.".... "The Bird will make sure that all things are put in their proper places on earth."

So this is how the beginning was made. Some call it the Creation.... [Today] if you enter the festival grounds and don't know your place, you seek out the head of the Bird Clan.... He will give you a direction and instruct you to seek out the head of [your] Clan and he will tell you exactly where to sleep.

Source: "Legends of the Seminoles," Seminole Tribe of Florida, <http://www.seminoletribe.com/culture/legend.s.shtml

Summary:

God created the animals and placed them in an eggshell. He told them that when the shell opened, they could crawl out and find their proper places on Earth. After the shell opened, the Wind helped the panther to come out first. Then all the other animals followed.

The Creator named the animals and put them into family groups. He told the panther that his family would be healers. The bird family would be in charge of putting all things on Earth in their proper places.

Even today if you don't know where to go at the festival to find your clan, the head of the Bird Clan will help you.

Vocabulary:

Clan = family group
companion = friend
festival = celebration

9

Summary:

God made a hole in the Sky, and pushed so many clouds through that they almost touched Earth. He stepped down the clouds and went far south. He knew that the Sun would be there to help him create the Real People.

God took a lump of clay and worked it into the shape of a man. He covered the man with leaves, and asked Sun to bake it for him. Sun went up into a tree and threw his heat toward the clay man, while God took a nap. When he woke up and uncovered the clay man, God saw that it was burned black.

He sent the black man away into the south and told him not to return without permission. Then God began to make another clay man. He asked Sun to sit farther away to bake this one.

Vocabulary:
fairly = completely
kneaded = worked with
    the hands
masses = piles; lots
plain = dry, flat land

Crow Story, Creation of the Indian

Great One came down from the Sky-land to the Earth-land one beautiful summer day. First, through a hole in the Sky-land he pushed down great masses of glorious white clouds, until they were piled up so high they almost touched the earth. Then he stepped through the hole, onto the cloudy heap, and took two long strides to clear the bottom. After he was fairly down, he went far south to a great wide plain, because here he was going to make the Real People. He went south, because Sun liked the south land better, and was there a great deal, and Sun was to help Great One.

Great One went to a great pile of clay which was heaped upon the plain and took a large lump of it in his fingers. He squeezed it this way and that, and rolled it, and kneaded it with his fingers until he made a man out of it. Sun had been watching him all this time. Great One covered the clay man with large leaves.

'Now, Sun,' said Great One, when the man was finished, 'sit up in that tree yonder and bake this man.' So Sun climbed up into the top of a big maple tree and threw all the heat he had toward that clay man. Great One took a nap. When he waked up, he went at once to the clay man and took off the leaves. Why, that man was burned black!

…Then [Great One] spoke to the black man. 'Go far into the south,' he said, 'Do not come up into this country again until I give permission….'

Great One began to make another man, while Sun wandered around for a while. When the next man was ready, Great One called to him, 'Ho, Sun! Go sit on that mountain top— that one far off—and don't send so much of your heat in this direction.' Then he covered the second man with large leaves so he would bake well, and took another nap.

Great One slept for a long time, and when he awakened, he rushed to the clay man and pulled all the leaves off in a great hurry. He didn't stop to think at all. And behold! The clay man was hardly baked at all. He was still white. Sun had sat too far away and had sent all his heat in another direction.

...So Great One gave him a canoe, and told him to go far off across the wide sea and not to come back until he gave permission.

Sun came up just then to see how things were going. They talked about the black man and the white man for some time. Then Great One said, 'Well! I'll make another man, and this one must be right, because my magic is almost used up....'

...[A]nd Great One made a third man and covered him all up with leaves. Then he stayed awake and counted up to five hundred while Sun sat up in the tree and sent just the right amount of heat out to bake that man properly....and behold! There was a red man—an Indian. He was baked just right, and he was just the kind of man Great One wanted.

Then Great One was very happy. He made a great many other men, and many women, and a few children. That is the way the Real People came to the Earth-land.... Great One never told any one about the black man and the white man, and the ... People knew nothing about them for a long, long time.

Source: Raymond Van Over, ed., *Sun Songs: Creation Myths from Around the World*. New York: New American Library, 1980, pp. 54–6.

Summary:

Sun went off to a mountain top, and God took another nap. When he woke up, he discovered that this clay man wasn't baked enough. He was still white.

God gave the white man a canoe, sent him off across the sea, and told him not to return without permission.

God and Sun talked things over. God decided to make another man, but said his magic was almost used up.

While Sun was baking the third man, God stayed awake and counted to 500. This man was baked just right.

God was happy, so he made more men, women, and children. They were the Real People. The people didn't know anything about the black and white men for a long time.

Vocabulary:
behold! = look!; observe!

Landscapes and Lifestyles

Thousands of years ago, Native Americans roamed the continent we call North America and lived off its rich resources. There were many Indian nations, and each one developed its own ways of living. Their lifestyles were influenced by the places where they lived—the weather, the terrain, the wild-life, etc.

In the Northwest, many tribes lived near ocean beaches or wide rivers. Some had both winter and summer homes. In this part of the country, the rich, damp landscape offered trees for building houses and canoes. Plants and animals were plentiful in the giant forests.

In the Southwest, some natives built cliff dwellings and stone houses from the easily carved rock. Others roamed the dry deserts seeking water and game. River beds carved into deep canyons invited Indian farmers to settle in the shelter of surrounding mountains.

The Indians of the Great Plains abandoned their shelters and villages to follow the buffalo across middle America. Their roving lifestyle brought them in touch with other wandering tribes, with whom they shared cultures and languages.

In the East, forests, marshes, lakes, and rivers offered a variety of game, plants, and fish. Here, tribes settled in large villages, where they developed farms.

Many of the earliest known tribes, which existed prior to the Europeans' arrival from the late 15th to the 17th centuries, are not well known today. Some assimilated with other tribes, but many were wiped out by diseases brought from Europe and by the white man's aggression toward them.

You may find many tribes that you do not recognize on the map to the right, because they no longer exist.

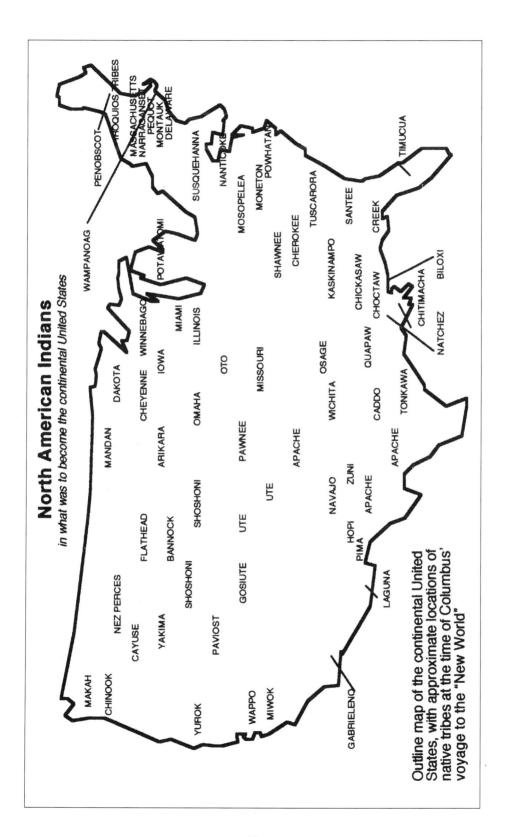

North American Indians
in what was to become the continental United States

Outline map of the continental United States, with approximate locations of native tribes at the time of Columbus' voyage to the "New World"

Homes

Native Americans used natural materials to build shelter from bad weather and to protect themselves from predators. For adobe homes, mud and grass were formed into blocks and baked in the sun. Animal hides became teepees. Other houses were made from logs, branches, and bark. In some areas, they carved out rock cliffs to make large caves and used stone to build large apartment-like structures.

Summary:

When I was a boy, we made tepees of buffalo skins. Rich tribal members had bigger tepees; poorer ones had smaller teepees. We counted our wealth by horses—and it took a lot of horses to set up a big teepee.

My father had the biggest tepee. Neighbors were afraid it would blow over on them.

Our teepee had two covers that could be pulled shut to protect us from wind and rain. The top was open for the passage of smoke. Snow would pile up around the outside and keep us warm. I liked listening to the rain come down on the tepee at night.

Vocabulary:

banked = piled; heaped
predators = animals or
  people that take from
  others

Description of Tepees
by Chief Luther Standing Bear (Sioux)

When I was a boy, all my tribe used tepees made of buffalo skins. Some were large, and others were quite small, depending upon the wealth of the owner. In my boyhood days, a man counted his wealth by the number of horses he owned. If a tepee was large, it took a great many poles to set it up and that called for a great many horses to move...

My father's tepee was the largest in our tribe. When we made camp, all the rest of the tribe would camp at a distance, as they were afraid the wind might get too strong in the night and knock our tepee over on them.

At the top of the tepee were two flaps, which served as windbreaks.... Our tepees were always set up facing east.

In case of rain, both flaps were closed down and tied to a stake driven in the ground. If a tepee was set up right, there was never any smoke inside, as the flue was open at the top. If snow fell heavily, it banked up all around the outside of the tepee, which helped keep us warm. On nights when there was a cold, sleeting rain, it was very pleasant to lie in bed and listen to the storm beating on the sides of the tepee.

Source: Chief Luther Standing Bear, *My People, the Sioux*, E.A. Brininstool, ed., Boston: Houghton Mifflin, 1928, p. 3.

Exteriors and interiors of earthen lodge and plains tepee (Franklin R. Johnston, *Life and Works Among the American Indians*, p. 59.)

Waheene: An Indian Girl's Story
by Waheene (Hidatsa)

The earth lodges that the Mandan and Hidatsa built were dome-shaped houses of posts and beams roofed over with willows and grass and earth. But every family owned a tepee, or skin tent, for use when hunting or traveling....

Source: Waheenee, *Waheene: An Indian Girl's Story.* Told by herself to Gilbert L. Wilson. St Paul: Webb Publishing Co., 1921, p. 9.

Summary:

The Mandan and Hidatsa tribes built curved-roof houses covered with willows, grass and earth. Every family also had a tepee for traveling.

Vocabulary:

beams = horizontal logs
    placed across posts
posts = vertical logs used
    as supports

Detail from "Pawnee women preserving corn," by contemporary Pawnee artist Alvin Jake (Found in Oliver La Farge, *A Pictorial History of the American Indian.* Bonanza Books, New York, 1966, p. 92.)

Summary:

On summer evenings, fires burned and women visited with one another. Families ate their meals. Old men sat and told stories. When a drum beat was heard, we danced almost every evening.

Vocabulary:

squat-on-heels = sitting on one's heels

yonder = ahead; farther away

Camp Life in the Early 20th Century
by Waheenee (Hidatsa)

Our camp on a summer's evening was a cheerful scene. At this hour, fires burned before most of the tepees and, as the women had ended their day's labors, there was much visiting from tent to tent. Here a family sat eating their evening meal. Yonder, a circle of old men, cross-legged or squat-on-heels in the firelight, joked and told stories. From a big tent on one side of the camp the tum-tum tum-tum of a drum. We had dancing almost every evening in those good days.

Source: Waheenee, *Waheene: An Indian Girl's Story.* Told by herself to Gilbert L. Wilson. St Paul: Webb Publishing Co., 1921, p. 9.

Food

Each Indian nation had its own favorite foods. The Apaches, who roamed the Southwestern desert, gathered plants such as cactus fruits. They also enjoyed meat from their hunts. The Pueblo, Hopi and Zuni people were farmers. They ate mutton from their herds of sheep, as well as beans, squash and corn from their gardens.

Native Americans also grew tobacco for use in cermonies. Corn was an important food, and legends were told about it.

"Hasjelti and Hostjoghon"
by Navajo storytellers

Hasjelti was the son of the white corn, and Hostjoghon the son of yellow corn. They were born on the mountains where the fogs meet. These two became the great song-makers of the world....

Other brothers were born of the white corn and yellow corn, and two brothers were placed on each mountain. They are the spirits of the mountains and to them the clouds come first. All the brothers together made game, the deer and elk and buffalo, and so game was created.

Navajos pray for rain and snow to Hasjelti and Hostjoghon. They stand upon the mountain tops and call the clouds to gather around them. Hasjelti prays to the sun, for the Navajos.

"Father, give me the light of your mind that my mind may be strong. Give me your strength, that my arm may be strong. Give me your rays, that corn and other vegetation may grow."

The most important prayers are addressed to Hasjelti and the most valuable gifts made to him.

Source: *Myths and Legends of California.* Found in Karin Luisa Badt, ed., *Indians of the Southwest.* Carlisle, MA: Discovery Enterprises, Ltd., 1996, p. 12-3.

Summary:

Hasjelti, son of white corn, and Hostjoghon, son of yellow corn, were born in the mountain fog. They became song-makers.

They had other corn brothers. Two of these brothers were put on each mountain, where the clouds come down. They made the deer, the elk, and the buffalo.

Navajos pray to Hasjelti and Hostjoghon when they want rain or snow. The brothers stand on moun-tain tops and call the clouds. Hasjelti prays to the sun and asks for warm rays to grow the corn. He is the most important brother and receives the best offerings.

Vocabulary:
plumes = large feathers
song-maker = prayer
  maker
vegetation = plants

Summary:

When I was young, our meat was sliced thin and hung in the sun to dry. It stayed good all winter. Cooked and dried strips of meat tasted like bacon. We also ate dried fruits, meat soup, hard-boiled eggs, and roasted fish and rabbits.

Vocabulary:
prairie = grassland; wide
  field

Preparing Food

This is about the food we ate when I was young. They used to slice the meat up thin and hang it up to dry in the sun. That way it would keep for the winter.... The meat from the back of the animal she cooked and dried. It was something like bacon.... We gathered wild grapes in the fall.... When I was a boy, living with my parents, we had dried meat and dried fruit for every meal. We used to have meat soup a lot, too. We ate hard-boiled eggs from wild turkeys and prairie chickens. Whenever we ate fish, they were cooked right in the ashes. Rabbits were roasted that way, too.

Source: Jim Whitewolf, *Jim Whitewolf: The Life of a Kiowa Apache Indian.* Charles S. Brant, ed., New York: Dover Publications, 1969, p. 50.

Summary:

The family meal was quiet and orderly. We ate on wooden plates. Soup was passed to us in large spoons made from horn. Mother decided how much each of us got, and we never asked for more. She put some food on the fire as a blessing.

Vocabulary:
portioned = distributed;
  dealt out

Family Meal

The serving of a family meal was a quiet and orderly affair.... The serving was done on wooden plates, the soup being passed in horn spoons of different sizes, some of them holding as much as a large bowl. The food was portioned to each one of us as mother saw fit, her judgment being unquestioned, for we never asked for more. Before serving us, however, mother put a small portion of the food in the fire as a blessing for the meal.

Source: Chief Luther Standing Bear, *Land of the Spotted Eagle.* Boston: Houghton Mifflin Co., 1933, p. 85.

Women at work in an Iroquois village, pounding corn and carrying firewood. (From a detail on a map by F. G. Bressani, 1657)

Water

In the dry, Southwestern desert, water was very important. Some Pueblo groups developed irrigation systems. Others, like the Hopi, depended on natural springs or streams. They carried water in large jugs on their heads. The Papago built small lakes near their homes. Many tribes performed rain dances and prayed to their rain gods.

Pima Rain Song

Hi-iya naiho-o! The earth is rumbling
From the beating of our basket drums.
The earth is rumbling from the beating
Of our basket drums, everywhere humming.
Earth is rumbling, everywhere raining.
Hi-iya naiho-o! Pluck out the feathers
From the wing of the eagle and turn them
Toward the east where lie the large clouds
Hi-iya naiho-o! Pluck out the soft down
   …and turn it
Toward the west where sail the small clouds.
Hi-iya naiho-o! Beneath the abode
Of the rain gods it is thundering;
Large corn is there. Hi-iya naiho-o!
Beneath the abode of the rain gods
It is raining; small corn is there.

Source: Frank Russel, *The Pima Indians.* Tucson: University of Arizona Press, 1975, p. 332.

Summary:

The earth echos from our beating drums. It hums. It is raining. Pull the feathers from the eagle. Point them to large clouds in the east. Pull the downy feathers and point them to small clouds in the west. Under the house of the rain gods, it thunders. Large corn grows. It rains. New corn grows.

Vocabulary:
abode = house; dwelling
pluck = pick; pull out
rumbling = echoing; growling

Hunting

In addition to the edible plants and fruits they gathered, Native Americans hunted animals for food. Animal hides and fur were used for clothing, shoes, saddles, and tepees. At first, the Indians hunted with bows and arrows, lances, harpoons, darts, clubs, slings, and other weapons. They tracked the game on foot. After the Europeans brought horses and guns, hunting became easier.

Most native people thought of animals as sacred. Dances and rituals are devoted to blessing the animals they had to kill in order to survive.

Summary:

First, I tried to shoot ducks. I loaded a shotgun, but was afraid to touch the trigger. So I tried to pull it with a stick. I switched to another gun and finally killed a rabbit. I learned to hunt by watching others; no one taught me how to do it. I never told my grandpa about my first time with the shotgun. I brought the rabbit home and my grandmother cooked it with bacon. My grandfather said, "Here comes the hunter with game." I became a good hunter. I used a shotgun, and I brought a rabbit home nearly every day. In the fall, they're good and fat.

A Klamath Man Remembers Learning to Hunt
by T. L. (Klamath)

First time, I started to hunt ducks first. I loaded a shot gun and there was lots of ducks. I was afraid to touch the trigger. I put it on the fence and tried to pull the trigger with a stick. Someway, I had to put it down. I was afraid. Finally, I took another gun. I was afraid to shoot but someway I touch the trigger and killed a rabbit. Then I wasn't afraid so I took the shotgun again. I became a good hunter. I learned by myself by watching other people. Nobody taught me. I learned by watching. I didn't tell my grandpa about that shotgun because he might think I am poor hunter. After I killed the rabbit I brought it into camp and my grandmother cooked it with bacon. My grandpa was pretty proud and told everyone, "Here comes hunter with game." Everyone was proud of me. After that, I came home with rabbit every day almost. Rabbits in fall is good and fat.

Source: Hiroto Zakoji, *Klamath Culture Change*. Master's thesis, Department of Anthropology, University of Oregon, 1953, p. 241.

George Catlin's painting, Comanchees Lancing a Buffalo Bull, around 1861 (Paul Mellon Collection)

Kiowa, The Buffalo Chase
by Old Lady Horse (Kiowa)

Everything the Kiowas had came from the buffalo. Their tipis were made of buffalo hides, so were their clothes and mocassins. They ate buffalo meat. Their containers were made of hide, or of bladders or stomachs. The buffalo were the life of the Kiowas.

Most of all, the buffalo was part of the Kiowa religion. A white buffalo calf must be sacrificed in the Sun Dance. The priests used parts of the buffalo to make their prayers when they healed people or when they sang to the powers above.

Source: Old Lady Horse (Kiowa), *American Indian Mythology*, Alice Marriott & Carol K. Rachlin, eds., New York: Thomas Y. Crowell Co., 1968.

Summary:

Buffalo were life for the Kiowa people. They used hides for tepees, clothes and moccasins, and ate the meat. They made bags out of the insides.

The buffalo was most important in their religion. They sacrificed a white calf in the Sun Dance. They used parts for healing.

Vocabulary:
bladder = the organ that holds urine
sacrificed = offered (usually killed) to please a god

Learning

In the early days, Native American children did not have formal schools, but their education was considered very important. In fact, it went on all the time. Just by being with their parents and elder tribal members, children learned to hunt, gather food, and to make warm and comfortable homes. By listening to stories, they learned Indian history, values, and traditions.

Summary:

Navajo children spent time outdoors. They learned about physical fitness, and ran hard races to build stamina. They shared family chores and cared for the animals. Girls worked with their mothers, who prepared wool, wove rugs, cooked Indian foods, and sewed clothing.

Vocabulary:

calicos = cotton cloth with patterns printed on one side

elements = weather; outdoor conditions

gleaned = gathered; picked up

stamina = endurance; health

techniques = methods; ways

traditional = common; handed down

Boyhood Education in the Early 20th Century
by Hoke Denetrosie (Navajo)

Young boys and girls were exposed to the elements. They learned the need for physical fitness, and they ran races at dawn and at noon when it was hot. This built stamina. Children were taught to help the family by sharing the chores and duties of everyday living. The boys learned to care for sheep, horses and other domestic animals. The girls learned to help their mothers in preparing wool and in using all knowledge and techniques necessary to the making of a rug, a task at which their mothers already had established themselves as expert weavers. They were taught the Navajo style of homemaking, including learning how to prepare many traditional foods which were grown in the fields, as well as those gleaned from natural sources. They were taught to sew and make traditional clothes from many colorful calicos and other materials that were bought at the trading post.

Source: *Stories of Traditional Navajo Life and Culture,* Navajo Nation, Arizona 86556. Arizona: Navajo Community College Press, 1977, p. 78.

A Santee Boy: Childhood Lessons
by Charles Eastman (Santee)

My uncle, who educated me up to the age of fifteen years, was a strict disciplinarian and a good teacher. When I left the teepee in the morning, he would say: 'Hadakah, look closely to everything you see'; and at evening, on my return, he used often to catechize me for an hour or so.

'On which side of the tree is the lighter-colored bark? On which side do they have most regular branches?'...

He did not expect a correct reply at once to all the voluminous questions that he put to me on these occasions, but he meant to make me observant and a good student of nature....

All boys were expected to endure hardships without complaint. In savage warfare, a young man must, of course, be an athlete and used to under-going all sorts of privations. He must be able to go without food and water for two or three days without displaying any weakness, or to run for a day and a night without any rest. He must be able to traverse a pathless and wild country without losing his way either in the day or night time. He cannot refuse to do any of these things if he aspires to be a warrior....

With all this, our manners and morals were not neglected. I was made to respect the adults and especially the aged. I was not allowed to join in their discussions, nor even to speak in their presence, unless requested to do so.

Source: Charles Eastman, *The American Indian: The First Victim*, Jay David, ed., New York: William Morrow & Co., 1972, pp. 72–3.

Summary:

My uncle was a good, strict, teacher. He taught me until I was fifteen years old. He made me observe everything I saw in nature and report back to him.

He didn't expect a correct answer to all his questions, but he wanted me to be a good student of nature.

All boys had to train to be strong. A young man must be able to fight fierce battles, live in the wilderness, and to go without food for two or three days. He must run for a day and a night and find his way in the light or dark. He cannot refuse if he wishes to be a warrior.

Our manners weren't forgotten. We learned to respect our elders.

Vocabulary:

catechize = teach; train
displaying = showing
neglected = ignored; unattended to
pathless = without paths
privations = hardships; troubles
savage = wild; brutal
traverse = travel; cross
voluminous = great number; many volumes

Playing

Like all youngsters, Native American children enjoyed playing games. Their toys often helped them to learn adult skills. Girls carried their cloth dolls on their backs, just like their mothers carried babies. Boys played with balls and sticks. They ran races that helped keep them fit.

Summary:

Cherokee children played with marbles made of baked clay. They also played a game with large beans. The beans were tossed in the air from a basket, and whoever caught the most won. Men and women played, too. The losers had to gather firewood for Christmas dinner. Winners rubbed soot on the losers' faces.

An important ball game had goals at either end of a playing field. The goals were about one hundred yards apart, similar to a football field. [Note: Cherokee families play these games today, to remind them of their ancestors' culture.]

Vocabulary:

leisure = free time
overtones = indirect hints;
    suggestions
political = related to
    community rules
saplings = young trees
smut = smear
soot = black ashes

Cherokee Games

Hardly any Cherokee was without marbles in his pocket. Made of pottery clay and hardened in the fire, they gave a person the chance to play and bet with his friends during leisure time....

The butterbean game was another pastime.... The game was played with six half-butterbeans, twenty four corn kernels as counters, and a flat basket about eighteen inches square and approximately two and a half inches deep.... A person put the six half-butterbeans in the basket, flipped them into the air, and caught them. Each flip that scored gave the scorer another turn.... The game brought people together for enjoyment.... On Christmas eve it was traditional for the men to play against the women. The losers gathered wood for the women to cook Christmas dinner. Winners were entitled to use soot to smut the losers' faces....

The ball-play, A-ne-tsa (little brother to war), was important to Cherokee people because it involved religious ritual and had political overtones.

Each team has two managers...who are responsible for making sure the few rules are not violated. The object of the game is to throw or carry the ball through a goal marked by two green saplings. The goals lie about one hundred twenty yards apart on flat open ground.

Source: Paul B. Hamel & Mary U. Chiltoskey, *Cherokee Plants And Their Uses—A 400 Year History.*

Green Corn Dance - Minatarrees, by George Catlin, 1861 (Paul Mellon Collection)

Religious Life

Native Americans believed in the power of nature, in souls, and in gods or spirits. They prayed, danced, sang, and expressed their wish to be in harmony with nature. Their medicine men were healers and religious leaders.

The Way to Rainy Mountain
by N. Scott Momaday (Kiowa)

There were frequent prayer meetings, and great nocturnal feasts. When I was a child I played with my cousins outside, where the lamplight fell upon the ground and the singing of the old people rose up around us and carried us away into the darkness. There were a lot of good things to eat, a lot of laughter and surprise. And afterwards, when the quiet returned, I lay down with my grandmother and could hear the frogs away by the river and feel the motion of the air!

Source: N. Scott Momaday, *The Way to Rainy Mountain*. The University of New Mexico Press, 1969.

Summary:

We often had prayer meetings and nighttime feasts. I played outside with my cousins and heard the old people sing. There was lots of food and fun. Later, I would sleep by my grandmother, listen to the frogs, and feel the night breeze.

Vocabulary:

feasts = large meals, celebration dinners

frequent = often happening

motion = movement

nocturnal = at night

25

Dancing

Dancers wore colorful costumes, and dancing was usually part of a celebration. Native Americans danced as a religious expression of gratitude for nature's blessings. Dances were also a way of asking for blessings in the future.

Summary:

Many dances are still used today. Cherokee women often danced too. The main reason for dancing was to teach us about our world. The dancers' masks were made of wood or other materials.

Vocabulary:

Booger = bogeyman; spook

Cherokee Dances

Dances remembered … are: Ball, Bear, Beaver, Buffalo, Booger, Eagle, Friendship, Green Corn, Partridge (Quail). The dances show us that Cherokee women often danced while their men danced, though seldom with them. [In] traditional Cherokee society…education surpassed recreation as a primary reason for dancing. Masks were usually made of buckeye wood or other materials that could be shaped quite easily.

Source: Paul B. Hamel and Mary U. Chiltoskey, *Cherokee Plants And Their Uses—A 400 Year History.*

Summary:

The Sun Dance is a dance of prayer. The dancer goes without water and food, and becomes dry, thirsty, hungry, and sleepy. Sometimes he has visions of the things that his people need. He brings these visions home to help his people.

Vocabulary:

do penance = accept hardship to show devotion
sacrifice = do without
visions = dreams; ghostly sights

The Sun Dance
by John Cummings (Crow)

When you go into a Sun Dance, you go out and pray.…When a man prays he should pray from the bottom of his heart, soul, body, and mind. You've got to sacrifice the water and the food. You might say you have to do penance…you get dry and you get hungry, you get tired, you get sleepy. And sometimes a man has visions of the good things that are needed in life, or his people's needs.…What visions they saw were brought home to help their people, not to ruin the people but to help the people to live, and that still exists today—that's what the Sun Dance is for.

Source: John Cummings, *To Be an Indian: An Oral History,* Joseph H. Cash and Herbert T. Hoover, eds., New York: Holt, Rinehart and Winston, 1971, p. 39.

Blackfoot medicine man. Face paint, necklace, and other decorations all relate to his magical powers. (American Museum of Natural History)

The Medicine Man

To the Indian, religion and healing were connected. Medicine men (a name used by white people) were holy healers who had a special knowledge of prayers, healing plants, and rituals used to cure sick members of the tribe.

From the Heart of the Crow Country
by Joseph Medicine Crow (Crow)

Who and what was this individual called 'medicine man' by the white man, *Wicasa Wakan* by the Sioux, *Batce Baxbe* by the Crow, and other names by other tribes?…He was made over thousands of centuries of gastronomical experimentation with unknown plants. Some killed him and some cured him, of course, but then he came through with good and practical knowledge of herbs that were best suited for relieving and curing his aches and pains.

Source: Joseph Medicine Crow, *From the Heart of the Crow Country.* New York: Orion Books, 1992.

Summary:
The healer was called by different names. Over hundreds of years, he tested many plants and learned which killed and which cured.

Vocabulary:
experimentation = testing; trying out
gastronomical = eating and drinking

Curing Ceremonies

Some Southwestern Indian groups, such as those who lived in Pueblos, held ceremonies where they prayed or danced to bring rain, good crops, or good hunting. Other groups, such as the Navajo and Apache tribes, held ceremonies for the health of a person. A shaman, or religious healer, performed a ritual and chanted to cure the patient.

Summary:

I live in nature's house, but there is a dark cloud at my door. Oh god! I make an offering of blessed smoke for you. Please make my feet, my legs, my body, and my mind healthy, as they used to be.

I am happy to be better. My insides feel cool and I no longer hurt.

May I walk as I walked long ago. May there be beauty all around me, everywhere.

Vocabulary:

deity = god
impervious = resistant
interior = inside
recover = get better
restore = bring back

Chant, Navajo Curing Ceremony

House made of dawn
House made of evening light
House made of the dark cloud
House made of male rain
House made of dark mist
House made of female rain…
Dark cloud is at the door…
Male deity!
Your offering I make
I have prepared a smoke for you
Restore my feet for me
Restore my legs for me
Restore my body for me
Restore my mind for me…
Happily I recover
Happily my interior becomes cool
Happily I go forth…
No longer sore, may I walk
Impervious to pain may I walk…
Happily may I walk…
Being as it used to be long ago,
    may I walk
May it be beautiful before me
May it be beautiful behind me
May if be beautiful below me
May it be beautiful above me
May it be beautiful all around me
In beauty it is finished.

Source: Karin Luisa Badt, ed., *Indians of the Southwest.* Carlisle, MA: Discovery Enterprises, Ltd., 1996, p. 24.

Ciguayos awaiting the arrival of Columbus and crew at Hispaniola. The Indians had never seen white men before. (Illustrated by Marion Eldridge, *Christopher Columbus and the Great Voyage of Discovery*, Discovery Enterprises, Ltd., Lowell, MA: 1990, p. 29.)

Changes

In the 1500s, strange new people began to arrive on Native American shores. It must have been something like the arrival of aliens from another planet would be for us today. The huge ships and the people with oddly pale skin were unlike anything the Indians had ever seen. The new people brought strange animals with them—horses, sheep, cattle—and powerful weapons. They moved onto Indian land. Their missionaries and settlers introduced new religions. The white people also carried new diseases, such as smallpox, measles, diphtheria, whooping cough, influenza, and perhaps yellow fever and malaria. These caused the deaths of many millions of Indians.

New People, New Places

The first meetings between the new people and the Native Americans were strange and frightening for both sides. They had no common language and had to use sign language as best they could. Some meetings were peaceful and led to the sharing of knowledge, food, furs, tools, and good will. Other meetings resulted in fierce battles.

Summary:

Long ago, before white men were here, some Indians were fishing. They saw something big floating far out on the water. They sent runners to tell their chiefs, who would call in the warriors. Later, they realized that the thing was moving toward them. They thought it was a large canoe or house carrying Mannitto, their Supreme Being. They prepared to receive their God with offerings and food. Although they felt confused—both hopeful and fearful—they began a dance. As the thing drew nearer, they could see that it was a floating house with many living creatures aboard.

Vocabulary:
Accordingly = in response
appeasing = soothing;
   satisfying
espied = saw
victuals = food; meals

Accounts told to John Heckler

*by Delawares, Mohicans, and other
Native Americans, about 1725*

A long time ago, when there was no such thing known to the Indians as people with a *white skin*, (their expression,) some Indians who had been out a-fishing, and where the sea widens, espied at a great distance something remarkably large swimming, or floating on the water, and such as they had never seen before. … Accordingly, they sent runners and watermen off to carry the news to their scattered chiefs, that these might send off in every direction for the warriors to come in. These, arriving in numbers, and themselves viewing the strange appearance, and that it was actually moving towards them…concluded it to be a large canoe or house, in which the great Mannitto (great or Supreme Being) himself was, and that he probably was coming to visit them.… Every step had been taken to be well provided with a plenty of meat for a sacrifice; the women were required to prepare the best of victuals; idols or images were examined and put in order; and a grand dance was supposed not only to be an agreeable entertainment for the Mannitto, but might, with the addition of a sacrifice, contribute towards appeasing him, in case he was angry with them. … Between hope and fear, and in confusion, a dance commenced. While in this situation fresh runners arrive declaring it a house of various colours, and crowded with living creatures.

Source: *Indian Tradition of the First Arrival of the Dutch at Manhattan as Related to John Heckwelder*, New York Historical Society Collection, 2nd. Series, I, c. 1765., pp. 71-4.

Accounts of the Old Ones
by First Boy

'There is a strange man walking towards the river with a gun on his shoulder,' [the scouts] said.... When he came closer, one from the party rose and walked towards him, at the same time lifting his hand as a sign for the man to stop. In sign language he was asked as to what tribe he belonged, but instead of an answer the man dropped his gun and raised his hands high above his head.

The rest of the party, when they saw the act, ran over and surrounded the man. Several spoke up, 'Don't any of you kill him, he is a different kind of man, let's look him over.'

He stood there terrified and continued to look from one to the other.

The man was tall and his hair was down to his shoulders. With the exception of his forehead, eyes, and nose, his face was covered with a heavy beard. His chest, his arms down to the tops of his hands, and his legs were covered with a hairy growth. Nothing like that had ever been seen among the tribe, only animals were that way.

'This must be what is called a white man, that we have heard about,' they said among themselves....

My granduncle took the man home and new clothing was made for him.... He stayed with our people for many years and my granduncle adopted him as a brother, because they were about the same age and height. He was named Lone White Man....

Source: First Boy, *The Assiniboines: From the Accounts of the Old Ones Told to First Boy,* Michael Stephen Kennedy, ed., Norman: University of Oklahoma Press, 1961.

Summary:

The scouts saw a man with a gun on his shoulder walking toward the river. One of the group went up to him and lifted his hand, telling the man to stop. He used sign language to ask the man what tribe he belonged to. But the man dropped his gun and raised his hands.

All the Indians gathered around. Some said, "Don't kill him, he is just different from us."

The man stood there in fear. His hair was long. And hair grew on his face, the back of his hands, his chest, and his arms and legs. They had never seen such a thing. Only animals looked that way. They decided this must be a white man.

My granduncle brought him home and made new clothes for him. He lived with them for many years and was known as, "Lone White Man."

Vocabulary:
granduncle =
    grandparent's brother

Summary:

The pierced-nose Indians are good-looking and dress well. Men wear white buffalo or elk robes decorated with white beads. Sea shells hang in their hair. They wear a decorated otter skin around their necks. Two bundles of brightly colored feathers hang forward over their shoulders.

Vocabulary:

beeds = beads
handsom = handsome; pretty

Summary:

The attacking Indians were the warlike Muscalleros [Apaches]. Their bows and arrows were powerful. The men are short but handsome, with yellowish skin and braided black hair. They wear buckskin belts, shirts, and moccasins. They look frightening when painted for battle.

Vocabulary:

complexion = skin tone; skin color
formidable = fierce; threatening
inclining = leaning toward
loins = thighs

The Journals of Lewis and Clark
by William Clark

October 10, 1805 Thursday

The Chopunnish or Pierced nose Indians are Stout likely men, handsom women and verry dressey in their way, the dress of the men are a White Buffalow robe or Elk Skin dressed with Beeds which are generally white, Sea Shells & the Mother of Pirl hung to the[i]r hair & on a piece of otter skin about their necks.... In two parsels hanging forward over their Sholders, feathers, and different Coloured Paints which they find in their Countrey Generally white, Green & light Blue....

Source: Bernard DeVoto, ed., *The Journals of Lewis and Clark*. Boston: Houghton Mifflin, 1953, pp. 246, 261-62.

Account of an Attack
by James Pattie

The Indians that attacked us, were a tribe of the Muscalleros, a very warlike people, although they have no other arms except bows and arrows, which are, however, the most powerful weapons of this kind.... The men, though not tall, are admirably formed, with fine features and a bright complexion inclining to yellow. Their dress is a buckskin belt about the loins, with a shirt and moccasins to match. Their long black hair hangs in imbraided masses over their shoulders, in some cases, almost extending to the heels. They make a most formidable appearance, when completely painted and prepared for battle.

Source: *The Personal Narrative of James O. Pattie*, printed in 1833, Library of Congress 66-26337, p. 117.

At Mesa Verde in Colorado are ruins of early Native American cliff dwellings. Above is a replica from the Mesa Verde National Park of what life must have been like for these Indians, long ago. One building, known as The Cliff Palace, has over 200 rooms and 23 ceremonial chambers.

A Report Made in 1582
by Pedro de Bustamente

They found a permanent pueblo with houses two stories high and of good appearance, built of mud walls and white inside, the people being dressed in cotton mantas [blankets] with shirts of the same. They learned that away from the river on both sides there were many other pueblos of Indians of the same nation, who also received them peacefully and gave them of what they had, namely maize, gourds, beans, chickens and other things, which is what they live on. Inquiry being made as to whether there were more settlements of people, by signs the natives replied in the affirmative.

Source: Herbert Eugene Bolton, ed., *Spanish Exploration in the Southwest.* New York: Barnes and Noble, 1908, pp. 142-50.

Summary:
There were two story, mud-wall houses painted white on the inside. The people wore white cotton blankets and shirts. Several other villages also received the explorers peacefully and gave them food. When asked, they signed that there were more Indian settlements in the area.

Vocabulary:
affirmative = positive, or "yes"
maize = corn; grain
pueblo = village

Captives

Sometimes Indians or settlers would take each other as prisoners. Some captives were treated well and others were not. In 1676, the Jamestown colony declared that Indian prisoners would serve as slaves. Some European prisoners told stories about suffering from hard work and even torture. Others were treated like members of the community. Mary Jemison was captured by the Iroquois in 1758, when she was fifteen. She lived comfortably with them until she died at the age of ninety.

Summary:

After I was captured, my clothes were badly torn. The women washed and dressed me in a new Indian outfit. Then they took me to a wigwam and sat me in the center.

I was very scared and certain they would kill me, but they were kind.

I was given a home and used as a nurse for the children. I also did some light housework. Sometimes I would go out with the hunters for short distances to help carry the game home. Life was easy.

Vocabulary:

employed = used; hired
squaws = Indian women
vengeance = revenge; anger

Autobiography Published in 1824
by Mary Jemison

The squaws…returned with a suit of Indian clothing, all new, and very clean and nice. My clothes, though whole and good when I was taken, were now torn in pieces, so that I was almost naked. They first undressed me and threw my rags into the river; then washed me clean and dressed me in the new suit they had just brought, in complete Indian style; and then led me home and seated me in the center of their wigwam.

During my adoption, I sat motionless, nearly terrified to death…expecting every moment to feel their vengeance, and suffer death on the spot. I was, however, happily disappointed….

Being now settled and provided with a home, I was employed in nursing the children, and doing light work about the house. Occasionally I was sent out with the Indian hunters, when they went but a short distance, to help them carry their game. My situation was easy; I had no particular hardships to endure.

Source: "Mary Jemison Becomes an Iroquois," in *Native American Testimony: An Anthology of Indian and White Relations, First Encounter to Dispossession*, Peter Nabakov, ed., New York: Thomas Y. Crowell, 1978, pp. 90-5.

Horses

Fifteen-inch-tall ancestors of modern horses lived on the American continents 55 million years ago. They died off long before people lived here. When the Spanish came to the Southwest, they brought horses with them. The Indians quickly adopted the new animals for travel, hunting, war, and companionship. The Indians expressed their love and admiration for their horses through songs and poems like the two below.

Navajo Song Honoring the Horse

My horse has a hoof like striped agate;
His fetlock is like a fine eagle-plume
His legs are like quick lightning
My horse's body is like an eagle-plumed
    arrow;
My horse has a tail like a trailing black cloud.

His mane is made of short rainbows.
My horse's ears are made of round corn.
My horse's eyes are made of big stars.
My horse's head is made of mixed waters.
(From the holy springs—he never knows
    thirst).
My horse's teeth are made of white shell.
The long rainbow is in his mouth for a bridle,
And with it, I guide him.

Source: Dane Coolidge and Mary Roberts Coolidge, *The Navajo Indians,* Boston, 1930, p. 2, The Horse.

Summary:

My horse's hoof is like a striped stone. His fetlock hair is like an eagle feather. His legs are quick; his body like an arrow; his tail like a black cloud. His mane is made of rainbows; his ears of corn; his eyes of stars. His head is water from the holy spring, so he's never thirsty. His teeth are white shell. I guide him with a rainbow.

Vocabulary:
agate = a type of stone
    with colored stripes
fetlock = joint that projects
    just above the hoof

Sioux Warrior's Song to His Horse

Anonymous

My horse be swift in flight
Even like a bird;
My horse be swift in flight
Bear me now in safety
Far from the enemy's arrows.
And you shall be rewarded
With streamers and red ribbons.

Activity:
Summarize this song
in your own words.

New Rules and Boundaries

As European settlers continued to move into Indian territory, the struggle for a place to live got worse. The Indians had lived on the land for a long time, but that no longer meant they had any claim to it according to the white man.

Summary:

The white man told the Omaha Indian not to come on his land. White Buffalo in the Distance pointed out that the white man enclosed his animals with a fence. But the Indians had wild animals that roamed the open spaces, so they needed to search for them.

Besides that, the Indian said, the President of the United States didn't buy this part of the land, so it's free.

The white man said he didn't care; he would fight to keep him off this land. White Buffalo in the Distance replied that he would go onto the land, and he would fight.

Vocabulary:

dwelling = home; living

sneering = scornful

stock = livestock; cattle, sheep

"Incident at Boyer Creek"
by an anonymous Omaha Indian, 1890

'I am unwilling for you to wander over this land,' said the white man.

White Buffalo in the Distance said, 'As you keep all your stock at home, you have no occasion to wander in search of them; and you dwell nowhere else but at this place. But we have wild animals, which are beyond our dwelling place, though they are on our land.'

'Though you say so, the land is mine,' said the white man.

'The land is not yours. The President did not buy it,…' said White Buffalo in the Distance.

'If the President bought it, are you so intelligent that you would know about it?' said the white man, speaking in a sneering manner to the Omaha.

'…Why do you consider me a fool? You are now dwelling a little beyond the bounds of the land belonging to the President,…' said White Buffalo in the Distance.

'Nevertheless, I am unwilling. If you go further, instead of obeying my words, we shall fight,' said the white man.

'I will go beyond. You may fight me. As the land is mine, I shall go,' said White Buffalo in the Distance.

Source: An anonymous Omaha Indian, "Incident at Boyer Creek" in J. O. Dorsey, *The Omaha Language.* Contributions to North American Ethnology, Department of the Interior, U.S. Geographical and Geological Survey of the Rocky Mountain Region, vol. 6, Washington, 1890.

Native Americans lost much of their land to the white man, and were horrified and saddened at the lack of respect they showed for nature. Unlike the Indians, who killed bison on the plains only for food, clothing, and shelter, the white man often slaughtered animals for sport and profit. As the buffalo began to disappear, some tribes were forced to relocate to the mountain regions, where they could hunt for deer. Where white "hunters" were known to kill a buffalo just to take its tongue or its horns as a trophy, the Indian made good use of every part of the animal, from the meat and the hide, to the teeth, bones, and marrow.

Black Elk Speaks
by Black Elk (Oglala Sioux)

I can remember when the bison were so many that they could not be counted, but more and more Wasichus [whites] came to kill them until they were only heaps of bones scatterd where they used to be. The Wasichus did not kill them to eat … they took only the hides to sell. Sometimes they did not even take their hides, only the tongues; and I have heard that fire-boats came down the Missouri River loaded with dried bison tongues. You can see that the men who did this were crazy. Sometimes they did not even take the tongues; they just killed and killed because they liked to do that. When we hunted bison, we killed only what we needed....

I could see that the Wasichus did not care for each other the way our people did....They would take everything from each other if they could, and so there were some who had more of everything than they could use, while crowds of people had nothing at all and maybe were starving.

Source: Black Elk, *Black Elk Speaks*. University of Nebraska Press, 1961.

Summary:

I remember when there were too many buffalo to count. Then white men came and only bones remained where the animals used to run. They killed them for their hides, or sometimes, just their tongues. Sometimes they killed just for the fun of killing. We only killed what we needed to eat.

White men did not seem to care about each other. They would steal from their own people. Even when they had plenty, they would let others starve.

Vocabulary:
bison = buffalo

Artist and historian George Catlin tried to understand the Native American. His paintings were intended to tell other whites more about Indian life. Above is Catlin's "Apache chief and three warriors," 1855.

Summary:

The Indians are in trouble because we are ignorant about them. We have done nothing but fight them and abuse them.

Vocabulary:

disposition = nature; personality

inducing = influencing; causing

misfortune = bad luck; unhappy situation

waged = carried on; fought

Letters and Notes on the North American Indians
by George Catlin

The Indians' misfortune has consisted chiefly in our ignorance of their true native character and disposition, which has always held us at a distrustful distance from them; inducing us to look upon them in no other light than that of a hostile foe, and worthy only of that system of continued warfare and abuse that has been forever waged against them.

Source: George Catlin, *Letters and Notes on the North American Indians.* New York: Clarkson N. Potter, Inc., 1975, p. 91.

Taking Control by Force

More and more settlers and explorers wanted to control the land. The use of force came early in the Southwest. In 1589 the Spanish invaded, searching for gold. Don Juan Onate, a Spanish leader, wanted to claim the Southwest territory for Spain. Onate and his men attacked the village of Acoma and killed many people. He then tortured the Acoma men as a lesson for other Indians in the area. In 1608, he established and ruled the town of Santa Fe, New Mexico. An excerpt from one of his letters follows:

1599 Letter
by Don Juan de Onate

The Apaches, of whom we have also seen some, are innumerable.... A few days ago I ascertained that they live like these in pueblos, one of which, eighteen leagues from here, contains fifteen plazas. They are a people whom I have compelled to render obedience to His Majesty, although not by means of legal instruments like the rest of the provinces. This has caused me much labor, diligence and care, long journeys, with arms on the shoulders, and not a little watching and circumspection; indeed, because my [man in charge of the camp] was not as cautious as he should have been, they killed him with twelve companions in a great pueblo and fortress called Acoma [Sky City], which must contain about three thousand Indians. As punishment for its crime and its treason against his Majesty, to whom it had already rendered submission by a public instrument, and as a warning to the rest, I razed and burned it completely, in the way in which your Lordship will see by process of this cause.

Source: *Spanish Exploration in the Southwest,* Herbert Eugene Bolton, ed., New York: Barnes and Noble, 1808, pp. 302-15.

Summary:

There are many Apaches who live in villages about three miles from here. I have conquered them, but not using official papers from the king. We have been at war. They killed my men who were camping out in the village of Acoma. As punishment, I destroyed it completely.

Vocabulary:

ascertained = discovered

circumspection = caution

compelled = forced

diligence = steady effort

innumerable = too many to count

instrument = method for getting something done

league = a distance of about three miles

razed = knocked down; destroyed

submission = yielding to the power of another

treason = betrayal to one's country or leader

War and Loss

Fighting between Native Americans and Europeans went on for more than 300 years. The wars finally ended in 1890, when the U.S. cavalry troops killed many Sioux at Wounded Knee.

Over the years, it could be hard to tell who was fighting on which side. At times, Europeans fought each other over land. Sometimes Indians would side with one group of Europeans and fight other Europeans.

Indians also fought with other Indians. Fierce Apache and Navajo tribes raided Southwest pueblos. Pueblo people turned to the Spanish for protection. Eventually, it became clear to Native Americans that they had lost the battle to control their homelands.

The Long Walk

In 1851, the U.S. built Fort Defiance in the middle of Navajo territory. Conflicts between the whites and the Indians were soon to arise. Manuelito, the Navajo chief, objected to the way the U.S. soldiers exploited grazing land that belonged to the Navajo. He and his men attacked Fort Defiance in 1860; skirmishes followed for the next three years. In 1863, General James Carleton, head of New Mexico's military, ordered the scout Kit Carson to push the Navajo off their land and onto a reservation in eastern New Mexico.

Although the Navajos resisted capture, hiding in the canyons, Carson's tactics, contaminating wells and burning crops, drove them to near starvation. In 1864, the Navajo surrendered and began the infamous three hundred mile Long Walk to the Bosque Redondo reservation.

Summary:

At first, we liked the Americans because they fought fair. Then they built a fort on our land and an agent wrote down promises for us to keep. We got lots of horses and sheep and were happy. But we had a fight with the Americans and we lost. We lost most of our land. We still had some beads and thought

continued on next page

Statement about the Navajo Defeat
by Chief Manuelito

...The Americans fight fair, and we like them. Then the soldiers built the fort here, and gave us an agent who advised us to behave well. He told us to live peaceably with the whites; to keep our promises. They wrote down promises, and so always remember them. From that on we had sheep and horses. We had lots of horses, and felt good; we had a fight with the Americans, and were whipped. At that time we thought we had a big country, extending over a great deal of land. We fought for that country because we did not want to lose it, but we made a mistake.

We lost nearly everything, but we had some beads left, and with them we thought we were rich. I have always advised the young men to avoid war. I am ashamed for having gone to war. The American nation is too powerful for us to fight. When we had a fight for a few days we felt fresh, but in a short time we were worn out, and the soldiers starved us out.

Then the Americans gave us something to eat, and we came in from the mountains and went to Texas. We were there for a few years; many of our people died from the climate. Then we became good friends with the white people. The Comanches wanted us to fight, but we would not join them. One day the soldiers went after the Comanches. I and the soldiers charged on the Comanches, but the Comanches drove us back, and I was left alone to fight them; so the white men came in twelve days to talk with us, as our people were dying off. He explained how the whites punished those who disobeyed the law. We promised to obey the laws if we were permitted to get back to our own country. We promised to keep the treaty you read to us today. We promised four times to do so. We all said "yes" to the treaty, and he gave us good advice. He was General Sherman.

We told him we would try to remember what he said. He said: "I want all you people to look at me." ...Then he said: "My children, I will send you back to your homes." ...we were so anxious to start.... When we saw the top of the mountains from Albuquerque we wondered if it was our mountain, and we felt like talking to the ground, we loved it so, and some of the old men and women cried with joy when they reached their homes....

Source: House Executive Document No. 263, 49th Congress, lst session, pp. 14-5.

we were rich. I am ashamed for having gone to war. The Americans were too powerful. They wore us out and starved us out.

Activity:
Continue to summarize this document in your own words.

In 1868, the Navajo were forced to sign an official treaty with the United States, giving up much of their land and agreeing to live on a reservation. Their children, according to the treaty, had to go to white schools. Below are excerpts from the infamous 1868 Treaty.

Activity:

Summarize this excerpt in your own words.

Vocabulary:

compel = force
cultivate = farm
discharge = carry out
implements = tools
induced = persuaded
pledge = promise

ARTICLE 1. ...The Government of the United States desires peace, and its honor is hereby pledged to keep it. The Indians desire peace, and they now pledge their honor to keep it....

ARTICLE 5. If any individual belonging to said tribe...shall desire to commence farming, he shall have the privilege to select, in the presence and with the assistance of the agent then in charge, a tract of land within said reservation, not exceeding one hundred and sixty acres in extent, which tract, when so selected, certified, and recorded in the "land-book" as herein described, shall cease to be held in common, but the same may be occupied and held in the exclusive possession of the person selecting it, and of his family, so long as he or they may continue to cultivate it....

ARTICLE 6. In order to insure the civilization of the Indians entering into this treaty, the necessity of education is admitted, especially of such of them as may be settled on said agricultural parts of this reservation, and they therefore pledge themselves to compel their children, male and female, between the ages of six and sixteen years, to attend school;...and the United States agrees that, for every thirty children between said ages who can be induced or compelled to attend school, a house shall be provided,...and a teacher shall be furnished, who will reside among said Indians, and faithfully discharge his or her duties....

ARTICLE 7. When the head of a family shall have selected lands..he shall be entitled to receive seeds and implements to the value of twenty-five dollars.

ARTICLE 8. ...the United States agrees to deliver at the agency-house on the reservation herein named, on the first day of September of each year for ten years, the following articles, to wit:

...articles of clothing, goods, or raw materials...not exceeding in value five dollars per Indian—each Indian being encouraged to manufacture their own clothing, blankets, & etc.; to be furnished with no article which they can manufacture themselves....

ARTICLE 9. ...the tribes who are parties to this agreement hereby stipulate that they will relinquish all right to occupy any territory outside their reservation, as herein defined, but retain the right to hunt on any unoccupied lands contiguous to their reservation...; and they, the said Indians, further expressly agree:

1st. That they will make no opposition to the construction of railroads now being built or hereafter to be built across the continent.

2d. That they will not interfere with the peaceful construction of any railroad not passing over their reservation as herein defined.

3d. That they will not attack any persons at home or travelling, nor molest or disturb any wagon-trains, coaches, mules, or cattle belonging to the people of the United States, or to persons friendly therewith.

4th. That they will never capture or carry off from the settlements women or children.

5th. They will never kill or scalp white men, nor attempt to do them harm.

6th. They will not in future oppose the construction of railroads, wagon-roads, mail stations, or other works of utility or necessity which may be ordered or permitted by the laws of the United States;....

7th. They will make no opposition to the military posts or roads now established....

Vocabulary:
contiguous = sharing a boundary, bordering
expressly = especially
relinquish = give up
stipulate = to guaratee in an agreement
to wit = namely

Consider this:
Many Plains Indians had resisted the white man's construction of the railroads. Explain your thoughts on why the Indians were attacking the trains which cut across their lands.

Which do you think was more important: That the Indians keep their hunting grounds and preserve nature, or that progress be made in transportation and communications? Explain.

ARTICLE 13. The tribe herein named, by their representatives, parties to this treaty, agree to make the reservation herein described their permanent home, and they will not as a tribe make any permanent settlement elsewhere...that if any Navajo Indian or Indians shall leave the reservation herein described to settle elsewhere, he or they shall forfeit all the rights, privileges, and annuities conferred by the terms of this treaty; and it is further agreed by the parties to this treaty, that they will do all they can to induce Indians now away from reservations set apart for the exclusive use and occupation of the Indians, leading a nomadic life, or engaged in war against the people of the United States, to abandon such a life and settle permanently in one of the territorial reservations set apart for the exclusive use and occupation of the Indians.

In testimony of all which the said parties have hereunto, on this the first day of June, one thousand eight hundred and sixty-eight, at Fort Sumner, in the Territory of New Mexico, set their hands and seals.

W. T. Sherman,
Lieutenant-General,
Indian Peace Commissioner.
S. F. Tappan,
Indian Peace Commissioner.

Barboneito, chief, his x mark
Armijo, his x mark
Delgado.
Manuelito, his x mark

[The treaty was signed by eight other Indian leaders, Council members, lawyers for the government, Army personnel, the agent for the Navajos, and others.]

Geronimo, photographed by Ben Wittick in 1887. (Arizona Historical Society)

Defeated Chiefs

One by one, the great Native American chiefs were defeated. The last Apache leaders surrendered in 1886. Hunderds of Apaches were sent to a prison in Florida. Many of their children were taken away to be raised by settlers.

Here is what Sitting Bull said when he was asked why he would not live on a reservation [land given to the Indians by the U.S. government]. At the time, he and his people were starving as they hid out in Canada.

Response to Questions
by Chief Sitting Bull (Sioux)

Because I am a red man. If the Great Spirit had desired me to be a white man he would have made me so in the first place. He put in your heart certain wishes and plans, in my heart he put other and different desires. Each man is good in his sight. It is not necessary for eagles to be crows. Now we are poor but we are free. No white man controls our footsteps. If we must die we die defending our rights.

Source: Sitting Bull, in Homer W. Wheeler, *Buffalo Days*, p. 253.

Summary:

Because I am a red man. The Great Spirit (God) created white men and red men to be different. To him, every person is good. We do not have to all be alike. Here, we are free. White man does not control us. If we must, we will die defending our rights.

Summary:

We always lived on our land. Our people had owned it as long as anyone can remember. Suddenly a white man came—the inspector.

He said, "The President of the United States says you must sell your land. He will pay you and give you new land in the Indian Territory."

We told him we didn't like the new land. We couldn't support ourselves there. We went to Washington to talk to the President.

In four days, we were home again. The inspector had already told our people to move. But the people wouldn't move until their chiefs returned.

The inspector told them that if they weren't ready to move tomorrow, they would be shot. Then the soldiers came, armed with bayonets.

Vocabulary:

bayonet = a blade attached to the muzzle of a rifle

inspector = a person whose job is to see that rules are being followed

A Personal Account
by Standing Bear

We lived on our land as long as we can remember. No one knows how long ago we came there. The land was owned by our tribe as far back as memory of men goes. We were living quietly on our farms. All of a sudden one white man came. We had no idea what for. This was the inspector....

The inspector said to us: 'The President says you must sell this land. He will buy it and pay you the money, and give you new land in the Indian Territory.' ...

We said to him: 'We do not like this land. We could not support ourselves. The water is bad. Now send us to Washington, to tell the President, as you promised.' ...

In four days we reached our own home. We found the inspector there. While we were gone, he had come to our people and told them to move.

Our people said: 'Where are our chiefs? What have you done with them? Why have you not brought them back? We will not move till our chiefs come back.'

Then the inspector told them: 'Tomorrow you must be ready to move. If you are not ready you will be shot.' Then the soldiers came to the doors with their bayonets....

Source: Helen Hunt Jackson, *A Century of Dishonor.* Boston: Roberts Brothers, 1893.

On the Reservation

For most Native Americans, life on the new reservations was very hard. They were used to living on the land in their own ways, and couldn't make the change to this strange new lifestyle. They were sad and depressed. Many became sick, and others starved.

Thoughts about the Reservation

by Cochise (Apache chief)

I came in here because God told me to do so. He said it was good to be at peace—so I came! I was going around the world with the clouds, and the air, when God spoke to my thought and told me to come in here and be at peace with all. He said the world was for us all; how was it? When I was young I walked all over this country, east and west, and saw no other people than the Apaches. After many summers I walked again and found another race of people had come to take it. How is it? Why is it that the Apaches wait to die…? They roam across the hills and plains and want the heavens to fall on them. The Apaches were once a great nation; they are now but few, and because of this they want to die…. Many have been killed in battle. You must speak straight so that your words may go as sunlight to our hearts. *Tell me, if the Virgin Mary has walked throughout all the land, why has she never entered the wigwam of the Apache? Why have we never seen or heard her?*

Source: Kansas State Historical Society Collections, Vol. 13, pp. 391-92.

Summary:

I came here because God spoke to me and said to do so. He said to be at peace, that the world was for us all. How was it before? When I was young I walked all over the land and only saw Apaches. Later, I met new people who had come to take the land.

How is it now? Why do the Apaches just wait to die? They roam their land and want the sky to fall on them. They were once great, but now are few. That's why they want to die. Many were killed in wars. You must speak honestly to us and bring light to our hearts. *Tell me, if the Virgin Mary has been here, why has she never come to us?*

Consider this:

Each Indian tribe had its own religious beliefs and customs. The white men wanted all Indians to become Christians. Should they have?

Summary:

Now I'm old. The animals are gone, and our Indian ways are almost gone. But I can't forget. In summer I get up early and slip out to the cornfields. I hoe corn and sing to it, as we used to. Now, no one cares about our songs.

As the sun sets, I look over the big Missouri river. I think I see our village, hear warriors yell, hear children laugh. But it's just a dream. There are only shadows and sounds of the river. Our Indian life is gone forever.

Vocabulary:
dusk = twilight; evening light
steal = slip; sneak

Summary:

An old Indian was forced to move to a house. They said his old tent was filthy. He looked weak, but he fought and they had to drag him out. He said he didn't want to live in a box.

Vocabulary:
feeble = weak
unsanitary = unclean
verminous = overrun with bugs or rodents

Waheenee, An Indian Girl's Story
by Waheenee

I am an old woman now. The buffalo and black-tail deer are gone, and our Indian ways are almost gone....But for me, I cannot forget our old ways. Often in summer I rise at day-break and steal out to the cornfields. And as I hoe the corn I sing to it, as we did when I was young. No one cares for our corn songs now.

Sometimes at evening I sit, looking out on the big Missouri. The sun sets, and dusk steals over the water. In the shadows I seem again to see our Indian village, with smoke curling upward from the earth lodges. And in the river's roar I hear the yells of the warriors, the laughter of little children as of old. It is but an old woman's dream. Again I see but shadows and hear only the roar of the river, and tears come into my eyes. Our Indian life, I know, is gone forever.

Source: Waheenee, *Waheene: An Indian Girl's Story*. Told by herself to Gilbert L. Wilson. St Paul: Webb Publishing Co., 1921.

"I don't want to live in a box..."
by Lame Deer (Sioux)

An old Indian ... was being forced to leave his tent and to go live in a new house. They told him that he would be more comfortable there and that they had to burn up his old tent because it was verminous and unsanitary. He looked thin and feeble, but he put up a terrific fight. They had a hard time dragging him. He was cursing them all the time: "I don't want no...house. I don't want to live in a box...."

Source: John Fire/Lame Deer and Richard Erdoes, *Lame Deer: Seeker of Visions*, New York: Simon and Schuster, 1972.

Afterword
by
Pat Perrin

During the 18th and 19th centuries, Native Americans lost a lot of their land. In the 20th century, new laws gave reservation lands back to Indian nations. They were granted limited powers of self-government. Some were repaid for lost lands.

During the 1950s, many federal programs for Native Americans ended. The government wanted Indians to join the larger society. However, that often meant economic disaster for Indians. Some aid programs were restarted in the 1960s.

In the 1970s, many Indians wrote and spoke powerfully about their people's problems. As a result, the U.S. made some more payments for land. And the Supreme Court has upheld the rights of Indians to fish or hunt on traditional lands.

On the reservations, education remains poor. Unemployment, suicide, alcoholism, and crime are higher than in the general population. Although many Indians moved to cities, they often lack the skills to make a living there. In recent years, some nations have started successful businesses, such as gambling casinos.

Now our Native American population is slowly growing. However, there's no exact definition of exactly who *is* an Indian. (The federal government requires proof of one-fourth or more of Indian ancestry.)

Especially in the Southwest, traditional Native American arts are still made. Indian basketry, weaving, and pottery are popular with collectors. Indian artists also work in more modern styles. And today's Indian authors have a wide audience for their books.

There's a lot more to be learned about Native Americans. Some cultures aren't even covered here. Those include the Arctic people called Inuits. You might want to learn more about a person or group that interests you.

Publisher's Note:
The web provides a good source of history sites and also has many sites on contemporary issues from Native American tribes. You should also be able to find much about Indian arts, music, and religions. You'll be delighted to see how many excellent books and museums feature Indian cultures, as well.

Research Activities/Things to Do

- With the arrival of Spanish explorers, life was forever changed for the Indians of the Southwest. Does the modern world owe the Indians restitution or is conquest just part of our history that we should learn to accept?

- Indian symbols such as the ones pictured below are often seen in rugs, baskets, weaving, etc. If you can find a hand-crafted item with symbols, try to interpret their meaning. Maybe a local museum has some items with graphic Native American symbols.

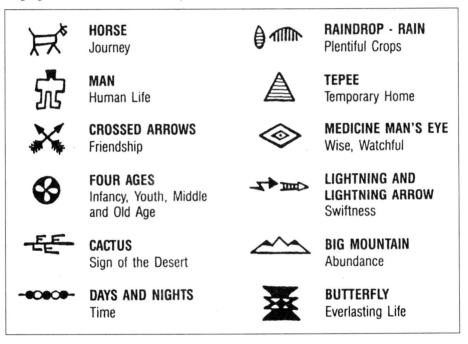

HORSE Journey		**RAINDROP - RAIN** Plentiful Crops	
MAN Human Life		**TEPEE** Temporary Home	
CROSSED ARROWS Friendship		**MEDICINE MAN'S EYE** Wise, Watchful	
FOUR AGES Infancy, Youth, Middle and Old Age		**LIGHTNING AND LIGHTNING ARROW** Swiftness	
CACTUS Sign of the Desert		**BIG MOUNTAIN** Abundance	
DAYS AND NIGHTS Time		**BUTTERFLY** Everlasting Life	

- Ancient Indian civilizations passed on their lore by word of mouth, from one generation to the next. They also recorded their history in cave paintings, sand paintings, and in the decorative symbols they used in their crafts. Early symbols are still found today in many Indian handicrafts and jewelry.

  Design a series of graphic symbols that relate to something which interests you, and then show how it might look when used in a craft item, such as a rug or a piece of jewelry.

- Show some examples of how nature played an important role in Indian legends. Take some contemporary political or social issue and retell it in the style of an Indian legend.

- In the 19th century, the loss of ancestral homelands caused by the white man's taking the land of the Indians occurred throughout the nation. As far west as the Washington Territory, the U.S. government forced the Indians onto smaller and more isolated reservations. Chief Seattle, a leader of several of the Northwest tribes, recalled in his speech to the governor of the territory:

  > "...There was a time when our people covered the land as the waves of a wind-ruffled sea cover its shell-paved floor, but that time has long since passed away with the greatness of tribes that are now but a mournful memory...."

- Is there any way to justify what the white man did to the Indians? Debate this issue with concrete examples from your research.

- Read the words of the Indian leaders below. Do you agree or disagree with them? Explain your answer.

"Hear me, Lakotas...before the ashes of the council fire are cold, the Great Father is buiding his forts among us. You have heard the sound of the white soldiers' ax upon the Little Piney. His presence here is an insult and a threat. It is an insult to the spirits of our ancestors. Are we to give up their sacred grounds to be plowed for corn? Lakotas, I am for war."

– Red Cloud, 1866

"I will remain what I am until I die, a hunter, and when there are no buffalo or other game I will send my children to hunt and live on prairie mice, for where an Indian is shut up in one place his body becomes weak."

– Sitting Bull, 1884

Analyzing Songs/Poems Worksheet

1. **Type of song document:**

   ❑ Sheet music   ❑ Recording   ❑ Printed Lyrics only

   ❑ Other_____

2. **Time period from which the song or poem comes:**

3. **Date(s) on Song:**

   ❑ No Date   ❑ Copyright

4. **Composer:**   **Lyricist:**   **Poet:**

5. **For what audience was the piece written?**

6. **Key Information** (In your opinion, what is the message of the song/poem?)

7. **Choose a quote from the piece that helped you to know why it was written:**

8. **Write down two clues which you got from the words that tell you something about life in the U. S. at the time it was written:**

9. **What is the mood of the music or poetry?**

10. **Does the wording have any "secret message" or symbolic meaning?**

The Cherokee

... Proud was his spirit, fierce, untamed and free
Scorning to crouch to pain, from death to flee:
With feeling suited to his savage state,
Faithful alike to friendship or to hate,
Seeking no meed beyond a warrior's fame,
And fearing nought except a coward's shame.

These wilds were his; amidst his chosen dell,
Where clustering wildflowers fringed the gushing well,
His hut was reared; and there, at closing day,
He heard his children's laughter-shout of play,
While, weary with the chase, his limbs were laid
In listless rest, beneath the oak tree's shade.

Then o'er the ocean-sea the white man came
Held to his lips the cup of liquid flame,
With smooth, false words, and bold encroaching hand,
Wrenched from the Cherokee his father's land,
Still on his fast receding footsteps prest,
And urged him onwards to the distant West,
'Till all the precincts of his narrowed ground,
Were closely hemmed with cultured life around;
And burning cottages and mangled slain,
Had marked war's footsteps o'er the ravaged plain.

Wearied, at length, the pale browed stranger swore,
To seek the Indian's hunting ground no more;
Treaties and oaths the solemn compact sealed,
And plenty crowned once more the blood stained field.
Then o'er the red men's altered nature smiles
A kindlier spirit, and a soul more mild;
Bright knowledge poured its sunlight o'er his mind,
His feelings softened, and his heart refined.
....
Then tell us, ye, who have the power to save,
Shall all his hopes be crushed in one wide grave?
Shall lawless force, with rude, remorseless hand,
Drive out the Indian from his father's land,
Burst all the ties that bind the heart to home,
And thrust him forth, 'mid distant wilds to roam?
Oh no! to mercy's pleading voice give ear,
The wak'ning wrath of outraged justice fear,
Stain not with broken faith our country's name,
Nor weigh her tresses to the dust with shame!
Remember yet the solemn pledge you gave,
And lift the potent arm, to shield and save!

Source: *Philadelphia Christian Advocate*, as printed in the *Cherokee Phoenix and Indians' Advocate*, June 5, 1830, Volume 111, Number 7. Also found in Madeleine Meyers, ed., *The Cherokee Nation: Life Before the Tears*. Carlisle, MA: Discovery Enterprises, Ltd., 1994, pp. 55-6.

Written Document Worksheet

Based on Worksheet from *Teaching with Documents*,
National Archives and Records Administration

1. **Type of document:**

   ❑ Newspaper   ❑ Diary   ❑ Advertisement

   ❑ Letter   ❑ Patent   ❑ Telegram

   ❑ Deed   ❑ Ship Manifest   ❑ Census Report

   ❑ Press Release   ❑ Journal   ❑ Memo

   ❑ Congressional Record   ❑ Report   ❑ Other_____

   ❑ Transcript from Oral History

2. **Unique Characteristics of the Document:**

3. **Date(s) of Document:**   ❑ No Date

4. **Author of Document:**   **Position:**

5. **For what audience was the document written?**

6. **Key Information** *(In your opinion, what are the 3 most important points of the document?)*

   a.

   b.

   c.

7. **Why do you think the document was written?**

8. **Choose a quote from the document that helped you to know why it was written:**

9. **Write down two clues which you got from the document that tell you something about life in the U.S. at the time the document was written:**

10. **Write a question to the author that you feel is unanswered in the document:**

Sample Written Document

The Dawes Act of 1887 forced Plains Indians to give up communal ways of life for individual family farms. Many Indians struggled to adapt to the new ways of life being dictated to them. But some, like Edward Goodbird, a member of the Hidatsa tribe in North Dakota, embraced the new order. In his autobiography, Goodbird describes subtle ways in which Indians managed to retain small aspects of their culture. Read, evaluate, and comment on the excerpt below:

"The White Man's Road is Easier!"
*A Hidatsa Indian Takes up the Ways of the White Man
in the Late Nineteenth Century*

Source: Edward Goodbird, as told to Gilbert L. Wilson, *Goodbird the Indian, His Story* (1914; reprint, St. Paul: Minnesota Historical Society Press, 1985), pp. 55-64. Found on http://historymatters.gmu.edu

The time came when we had to forsake our village at Like-a-fish-hook Bend, for the government wanted the Indians to become farmers. "You should take allotments," our agent would say. "The big game is being killed off, and you must plant bigger fields or starve. The government will give you plows and cattle."

All knew that the agent's words were true, and little by little our village was broken up. In the summer of my sixteenth year nearly a third of my tribe left to take up allotments.

We had plenty of land; our reservation was twice the size of Rhode Island, and our united tribes, with the Rees who joined us, were less than thirteen hundred souls. Most of the Indians chose allotments along the Missouri, where the soil was good and drinking water easy to get. Unallotted lands were to be sold and the money given to the three tribes.

Forty miles above our village, the Missouri makes a wide bend around a point called Independence Hill, and here my father and several of his relatives chose their allotments. The bend enclosed a wide strip of meadow land, offering hay for our horses. The soil along the river was rich and in the bottom stood a thick growth of timber.

My father left the village, with my mother and me, in June. He had a wagon, given him by the agent; this he unbolted and took over the river piece by piece, in a bull boat; our horses swam.

We camped at Independence in a tepee, while we busied ourselves building a cabin. My father cut the logs; they were notched at the ends, to lock into one another at the corners. A heavier log, a foot in thickness, made the ridge pole. The roof was of willows and grass, covered with sods.

Cracks between the logs were plastered with clay, mixed with short grass. The floor was of earth, but we had a stove.

We were a month putting up our cabin.

Though my father's coming to Independence was a step toward civilization, it had one ill effect: it removed me from the good influences of the mission school, so that for a time I fell back into Indian ways.

- Do some research on some of the early Indian raids and kidnappings in New England towns. Why did some of the kidnapped women and children choose to remain with the tribes who had captured them, rather than returning to their homes?

- Indians told their tribal and family histories by passing along their stories from one generation to the next, orally. How accurate was this method? What problems may have arisen when later historians tried to interpret Native American history? Explain.

- To simulate the ordeal of the "Long Walk" of the Apaches and Navajos in 1864, plan a walk in your school. Carry all of the things you feel you must take with you (or never see again), and start walking at the beginning of the school day, right until dismissal (around a track, or in circles around the school itself). As the day wears on—rain or shine—see how much of the stuff you thought you needed to bring, you have decided to leave along the way, to ease your burden. The Indians were forced to walk over 300 miles. How far did you get in a day?

Suggested Further Reading

There are many excellent novels that relate to Native American history and legend. Following are a few recommended titles which may be of interest:

* *The Girl Who Chased Away Sorrow, Diary of Sarah Nita, Navajo Girl*, Ann Turner - El
* *Where The Broken Heart Still Beats: The Story of Cynthia Ann Parker*, Carolyn Meyer (Comanche) - M
* *Moccasin Trail*, Eloise Jarvis McGraw (Crow) - M
* *Bearstone*, Will Hobbs - M
* *Sing Down the Moon*, Scott O'Dell (Navajo) - M
* *Save the Queen of Sheba*, Louise Moeri - M
* *Cherokee Trail*, Lewis L'Amour - HS

El = elementary level
M = middle school level
HS = high school level